AN EARLY LUNCH IS A GOOD DECISION AT LEAST SIXTY PERCENT OF THE TIME

P.T. Collis

BookLeaf Publishing

India | USA | UK

Presentation by BookLeaf Publishing

Web: www.bookleafpub.com

E-mail: info@bookleafpub.com

ISBN: 9789358360257

First edition 2021

ACKNOWLEDGEMENT

I would like to acknowledge the Wurundjeri people of the Kulin nation who are the traditional custodians of the land on which these poems were written.

Sovereignty was never ceded.

The poems contained within this book were primarily completed while avoiding the responsibilities of nine-to-five living.

I dedicate this to Christine, whom I love the most.

Chicken bones and quinoa salad

Do not talk about yesterday's match

From the empty seats

In the lunchroom

A half-drunk mug of lukewarm coffee

Does not dissect

The premier's morning presser

They do not talk about

The milquetoast events

That filled their weekend past

And they do not feign interest

In mine

In the last twelve months

I have discovered that

An early lunch is a good decision

At least sixty percent of the time

Do you think she'll come tonight?

Do you think she'll come

For that pale moonlight?

For the rising sun?

Do you think she'll come?

Is she happy keeping safe

Where the water is warm?

Where there's naught to face?

White coat holding proud

With that sanguine air

Sings so assured

O he thinks she might

If not this morn

Then morrow's night

The necklace says

That she's beating fine

On her dawning drum

Now today is done

Do you think she'll come?

Would it suit me ill

To stand in a field

With some tattered clothes

And scare away crows?

Am I damned if I do

Like I am when I don't?

I don't know how light works

I don't understand matter nor stars

and I don't know how the wind blows

or why

I do not know

what the moon has to do with the tide

that crashes constantly into the shore

or why those plates beneath us dance slowly

not cheek-to-cheek

but with two left feet

and I do not know why

some choose to believe

they are more worthy

based purely on the time and place

and from whom they happened to be birthed

that they first screamed

still attached and wet with mother's membrane

when the moon was high

and the light of day unseen

concluding that the sun must rise for them

and them alone

and I cannot understand

why coriander is so despised

nor what genes may have to do with it

but I know that when I've made pico de gallo

and I'm slicing avocado with my love

to delicately place atop some tortillas

with spiced vegetables and cheese and chilli

(or whatever else is in the fridge)

I don't tend to wonder if hatred is hereditary

One foot down

And then the next

Is harder than it

Has any right to be

Distressed is the varnish

On the corners of the slats

That face the tracks

At Box Hill Station

I sit

Like millions of others before me

On the edge of their seats

In wait of a train

On a late April morn

I am alone in my colours

I am not alone in the waiting

And I am not alone in a smile

As a stranger passes

Soft serve in hand

Though winter knocks

with early earnest

It does not melt.

Not onto her coat

Not onto her boots

And the polyanna I keep in my pocket

Insists it would not

Not even if the air were sufficiently warmed

Later, I'm standing in line

For the bathrooms at half-time

Where my tribe is down

I am familiar with the blue in my colours

For the ferocity expected

Is insufficient indeed

I will say to most that I don't mind the losses

If our best is given

And we can hold our head high

Though it aches with effort

And our hands and legs shake

And our breathing deepens and quickens

And we wear all of our pain

With some goddamn pride

Occasionally I even mean it

Then I return to my seat

And I think of ice cream

And I think of my friend beside

With whom I have shared

A great many questionable decisions

Including, but not limited to,

The team that we choose to support

His face and eyes and mind converse

with a pocket computer

And he asks how my evening will look

I could not tell you

the difference in points

Nor which of the lawmen I disagreed with most

I can tell you

The rain was heavy on Elizabeth Street

Where my friend and I drank beer

Speaking of dreams and heartache

Of sepia toned memories

Of future plans

Of strangers, tattoos

Of how to turn sweet potato and flour into bread

over spicy fried chicken

Before we entered the arena

To heckle some athletes

Before afternoon turned to evening

And then into night

And then into morn again

When my love, she calls to ask

If she should keep the side door open

Or if I remembered my keys this time

I escape

From my cubicle

To a different cubicle

Beneath a white light

Fluorescent and sterile

Where the walls

are much closer

but do not close in

Where a sticky-taped sign

on the door's back requests

That I use the brush

Where I am somehow less likely to be caught

With my pants down

Or my dick in my hand

It's times like these

That I miss the comfort of the cold rain

A thick scratchy sweater

And something that might give me cancer

Or at least make my breath smell

Jo had the fall from her bed

In the home where she slept

And she sat and existed

Never the one to complain

She praised sunshine and rain

Between bingo and biscuits

But her hands were shaky

And her bones were aching

Mistook puzzle pieces

For faces and names

The walk to her room

A march atop a moving train

I shed my tears by the bins with a cigarette

Counting the crows lining up on the fence

With respects and condolences

Memories of seed in a bowl

And her smile

when the Bloods won the Premiership

Her name was Jocelyn

But folks call me Josie, she said

She was my grandmother

And now she is dead

Do not ask me why

For I do not know

But in the back of my mind

I thought that nobody kept gargoyles

On the roofs of their houses anymore

That is something I'd like to see come back

Let's make manors creepy again

So I can call upon my friends

And tell them that it's full of vampires

And we could ride together on our bicycles

With pitchforks and torches

In violent nostalgia

And neighbourhood pride

I will never be part of the clubs

That make that gargoyle coin

My blood doth lack the richness

It is unpleasant on the tongue

And the clubs are wise

So very, very wise

Not to want me

Dear Salespeople,

I do not make enough money

to help you meet your KPIs.

Please stop calling me.

That's it.

That's the poem.

There is a frog

in the throat

of the body

that I drive

at the office

in the house

where I snack

and enter data

and while I do

I watch people

get eaten

by zombies

or bisected

by maniacs

and the day

it moves

so slowly

and the evening

approaches

at insufficient speed

and somewhere

over a fence

a dog

is barking.

At the window

watching planes

flying between

the clouds and rain

Do you recall

when last you woke

without resentment

feeling safe?

Don't I know you?

I could have sworn you called me darling

Back when cheap red tasted better

And we could sleep all night

in the backseat of my car

And wake without neck pain

But to a smile that would put the sun to shame

Until I held a half-empty pint like a shield

And ate my words by the spoonful

I am happy not hearing you speaking my name

Or standing beside me

As we laugh at the faces in renaissance paintings

She does not need to tell me

That she is more comfortable in what is mine

When I catch her dancing in the kitchen

Sporting that holey old pair of trunks

And the button-up I dropped on the floor last night

She cannot sneak into a room.

The cool click of her heels

And the scent her perfume dances with

Are not unnoticed by the air

Who calls to all that it can reach

Lest they miss something incredible

Luna, daughter of Theia and Earth,

Dangles drunk between candles,

With a belly of silica, iron, and lime,

And reminds us that the Sun is shining

Even when it does not shine

Upon our shoulders

Even though it's legal now

I do not trust the folks that live beyond my house

And I am sceptical of leaving it myself

Or letting them trust me

The advertisers tell me that past performance

is not an indicator of future performance.

I do not blame the magpie

Who swoops pre-emptively

As I near their kin

I am, after all,

Half-British

And a white Australian

19

Clothes in the garden catch rain on a string

Birds collect pollen now the bees learnt to sing

Knots in the timber look a lot like my dad

When I said I forgave him, they stared right back

The lenses aren't rosy, but the frame's plated gold

You did what you could when you did, I suppose

20

My Simple Rick moment

Is that look she gives me

When she is swaying to Etta James

Over a bowl of pancake batter

I slide my hands

From her shoulders, slow

Down her arms

They kiss her elbows

(and my lips, her neck)

When they meet her hips

She vibrates

And the air is changed

Then she turns

She lays the bowl down gently

And she rests her arms on my shoulders

And the corners of her mouth

Pull the curtain to a smile

And her eyes beam into mine

Welcomed to life

A technicolour dream

When she gives me

That Look

I am the butter atop the pancake stack